No, Thank You

By Janine Amos   Illustrated by Annabel Spenceley

Gareth Stevens Publishing
A WORLD ALMANAC EDUCATION GROUP COMPANY

Please visit our web site at: www.garethstevens.com
For a free color catalog describing Gareth Stevens'
list of high-quality books and multimedia programs,
call 1-800-542-2595 (USA) or 1-800-461-9120 (Canada).
Gareth Stevens Publishing's Fax: (414) 332-3567.

Library of Congress Cataloging-in-Publication Data

Amos, Janine.
    No, thank you / by Janine Amos; illustrated by Annabel Spenceley.
       p. cm. — (Courteous kids)
    Includes bibliographical references.
    ISBN 0-8368-2805-4 (lib. bdg.)
    1. Courtesy—Juvenile literature. 2. Children—Conduct of life.
  [1. Etiquette. 2. Conduct of life.] I. Spenceley, Annabel, ill. II. Title.
BJ1533.C9A465   2001
395.1'22—dc21   00-049297

This edition first published in 2001 by
Gareth Stevens Publishing
A World Almanac Education Group Company
330 West Olive Street, Suite 100
Milwaukee, WI 53212 USA

Gareth Stevens editor: Anne Miller
Cover design: Joel Bucaro

This edition © 2001 by Gareth Stevens, Inc. First published by Cherrytree Press,
a subsidiary of Evans Brothers Limited. © 1999 by Cherrytree (a member of the
Evans Group of Publishers), 2A Portman Mansions, Chiltern Street, London
W1M 1LE, United Kingdom. This U.S. edition published under license from
Evans Brothers Limited. Additional end matter © 2001 by Gareth Stevens, Inc.

Printed in the United States of America

1 2 3 4 5 6 7 8 9 05 04 03 02 01

Snack Time

Everyone had a piece of cake at snack time.
Mom offers Amy a second piece.

Mom offers another piece to Jeff.
Amy and Jeff forget to say "thank you."

7

How does Mom feel?

Mom offers more cake to Rosalie.

9

Rosalie smiles and says, "No, thank you."

How does Mom feel now?

Too Busy!

Nathan is drawing space rockets.

Josh is looking for someone to play with.

Nathan is too busy. He says, "No."
He forgets to say, "Thank you."

How does Josh feel?

Josh asks Sammy to play with him.

Sammy is busy, too.
He smiles and says, "No, thank you."

How does Josh feel now?

Tina and Mai

Tina is building a tower.

It's wobbly! The tower starts to fall.

Mai comes over to help.

But Tina wants to do it herself.

How does Mai feel?

Tina forgot to say "thank you."

Then she remembers.

How does Mai feel now?

More Books to Read

The Berenstain Bears Forget Their Manners. Stan Berenstain and
  Jan Berenstain (Econo-clad Books)

Elmo's Good Manners Game. Catherine Samuel
  (CTW Books)

Manners. Aliki (Greenwillow)

Saying No. Let's Talk About (series). Joy Berry (Scholastic)

Note to Parents and Teachers

The questions that appear in **boldface** type can be used to initiate
discussion with your children or class. Encourage them to think of
possible answers before continuing with the story.

Additional Resources

Parents and teachers may find these materials useful in discussing
manners with children:

Video: *Manners Can Be Fun!* (ETI-KIDS, Ltd.)
  This video includes a teacher's guide.

Web Site: *Preschoolers Today: Where Have the Manners Gone?*
  www.preschoolerstoday.com/resources/articles/manners.htm